ACTION HEROES

THE CREATION OF IRON MAN®

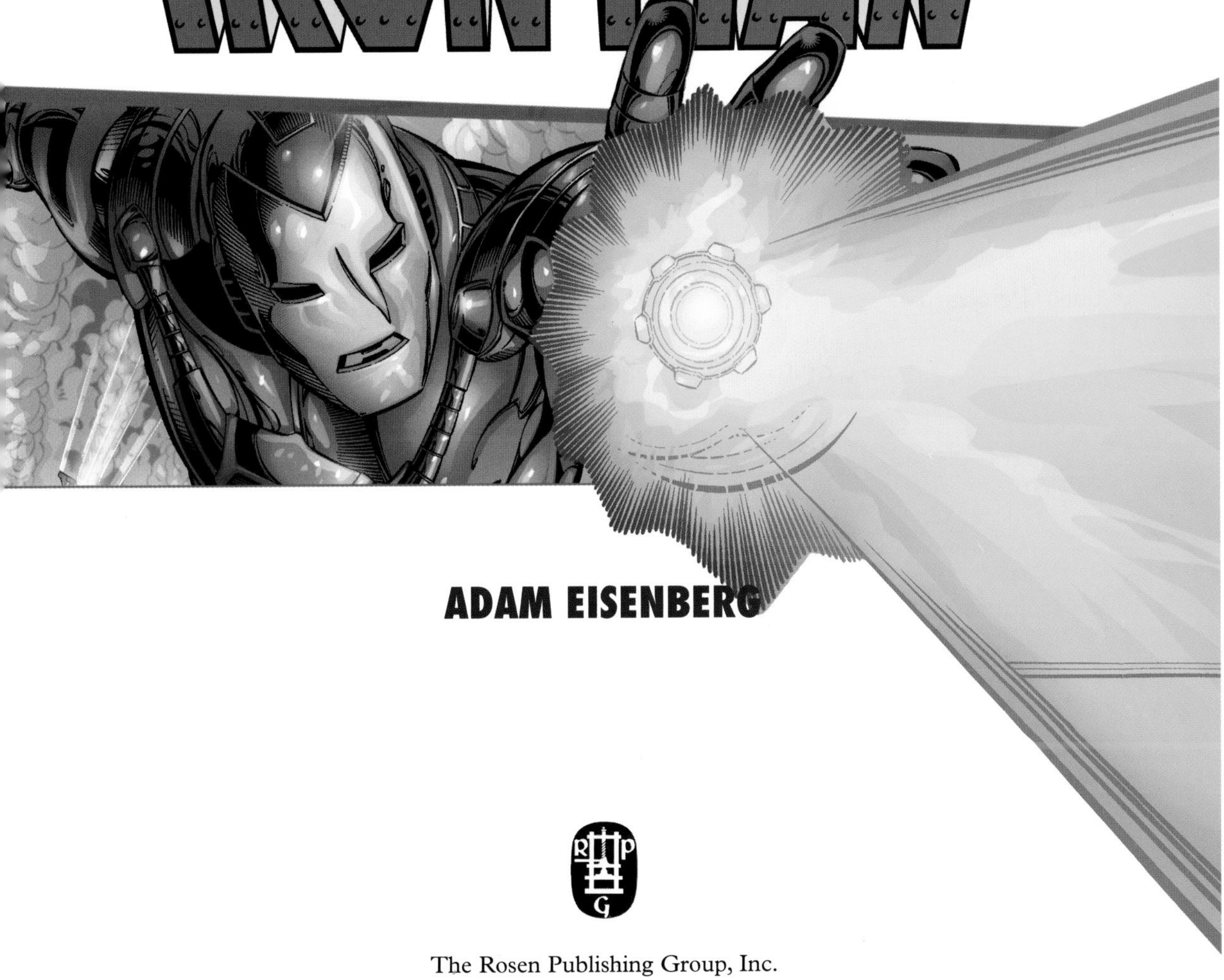

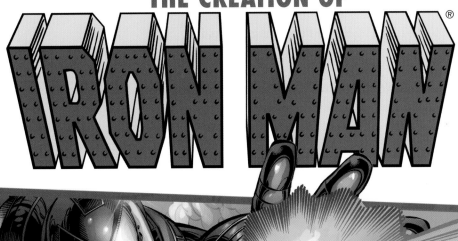

ADAM EISENBERG

The Rosen Publishing Group, Inc.
New York

For my mom

Published in 2007 by The Rosen Publishing Group, Inc.
29 East 21st Street, New York, NY 10010

Copyright © 2007 by The Rosen Publishing Group, Inc.
First Edition

Thanks to Marvel Entertainment, Inc.: Avi Arad, James Hinton, Mary Law, Bruno Maglione, Tim Rothwell, Mickey Stern, Alberta Stewart, and Carl Suecoff

Library of Congress Cataloging-in-Publication Data

Eisenberg, Adam.
The creation of Iron Man/by Adam Eisenberg.—1st ed.
    p. cm.—(Action Heroes)
Includes bibliographical references and index.
ISBN 1-4042-0767-8 (lib. bndg.)
1. Iron Man (Fictitious character) I. Title. II. Series.
PN6728.I76E47 2006
741.5'973—dc22

                                                                2006000167

Manufactured in the United States of America
On the cover: Iron Man flies in a version of armor created for the Heroes Return series. It features modern conveniences for fighting crime, including a built-in cell phone, digital camera, and wireless modem for connecting to the Internet.
Title page: Iron Man's magnetic repulsor beam can be fired like a laser. It allows Iron Man to control objects and create a protective shield strong enough to block gunshots.

CONTENTS

INTRODUCTION 5

1 JACK AND STAN 8

2 DIFFERENT HEROES FOR A DIFFERENT GENERATION 13

3 THE MAN IN THE METAL SUIT 20

4 IRON FANS 29

5 IRON INFLUENCE 36

TIMELINE: STAN LEE AND JACK KIRBY 40

IRON MAN HIGHLIGHTS 41

GLOSSARY 42

FOR MORE INFORMATION 43

FOR FURTHER READING 44

BIBLIOGRAPHY 45

INDEX 47

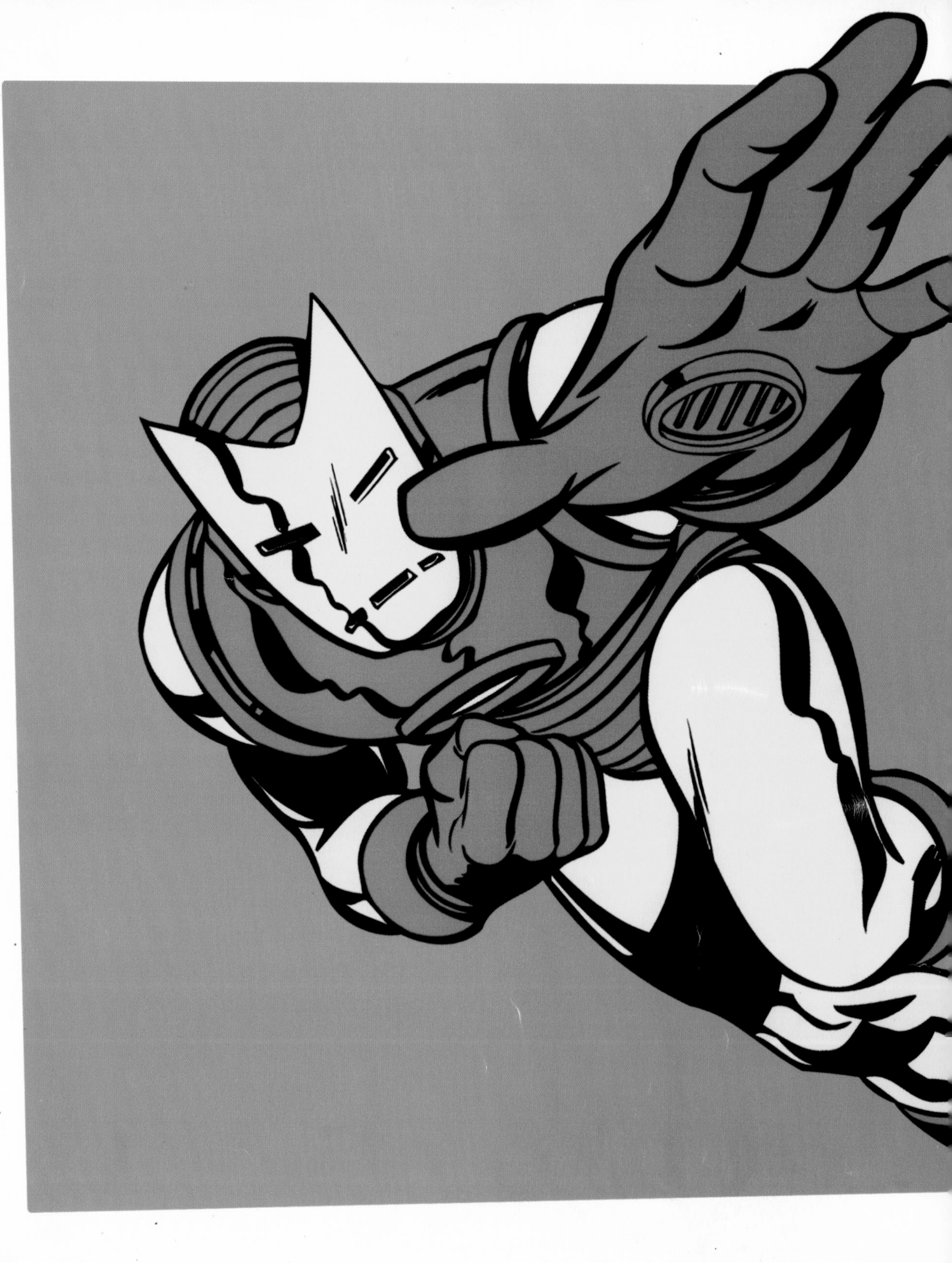

INTRODUCTION

His rocket-propelled boots allow him to fly high above the skyline. He wears a suit of armor so powerful that a thousand swings from the world's hardest-hitting baseball team couldn't put a dent in him. He can control metal objects, electricity, and light with the energy generated from his suit. He is capable of defeating alien invaders, criminal master-minds, and deadly robots. About the only thing the invincible Iron Man can't do is lead a normal life.

Born in the pages of Marvel Comics in 1963, Iron Man (Tony Stark when he wasn't in Super Hero form) was not a typical Super Hero. Like many of the characters created by Marvel Comics in the early 1960s, Iron Man's powers allowed him to do amazing things, but they also led to tragic results. From failed relationships to harmful thieves using his inventions, Iron Man often had more to deal with than saving New

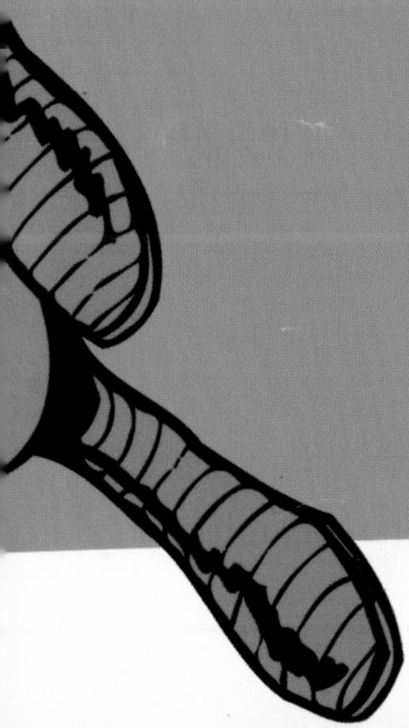

York City from the Mandarin's deadly rings or the Crimson Dynamo's laser ray gun. First published in 1968, *The Invincible Iron Man* was one of Marvel's most popular and longest-running Super Hero comics. Like most of the Marvel titles from the time period, it was the character development as well as the action-soaked pages that hooked the fans.

Iron Man's success was the result of a unique working relationship between Jack Kirby and Stan Lee, two of the most important figures in comic book history. Together, they produced what is now known as the Marvel Universe, and they transformed the way people thought about superhero comics. Neither Lee nor Kirby set out to change comic books, but by the time they co-created Iron Man, they were well on their way to making some of the most significant contributions in the medium's history. There were high and low points throughout the many years they worked in the industry. At times, they were ready to give up on comic books for good. Although they spent only a few years working together, those years produced the most famous work of either of their careers. With Kirby's groundbreaking art and imagination, and Lee's catchy dialogue, their characters looked, talked, and acted more like regular people with regular problems than previous superheros. The characters could burst into flames or control objects with their minds, but they had to deal with everyday things as well, like paying the rent and getting their cars washed.

Iron Man confronted mythological and supernatural villains, but the comic books were also about war. Battles were both real and imagined, and often reflected the politics and social attitudes of the day. *Iron Man* confronted the Vietnam War and, more recently, the First Gulf War.

Iron Man, or "Shell Head" as Stan Lee likes to call him, continuously changed with the times. Few Super Heroes or Super Villains in the history of comics have worn as many different outfits or used the variety of weapons, devices, and gadgets as Iron Man. He started out wearing a clunky gray suit and, in time, came to resemble a streamlined, high-tech machine. Later, his wires were ditched for microchips, and satellites replaced his antennas.

Regardless of what outfit he wore, the technology he used, or the politics of the day, what made Iron Man a unique character were his problems. He could smash a ten-ton robot or deflect a laser beam, but meeting a friend for dinner or acting like a regular guy was always the real challenge.

1 JACK AND STAN

Although they worked together to co-create Iron Man, Stan Lee and Jack Kirby's personalities were as different as salt and sugar. Lee is tall and lanky with a permanent grin attached to his face. Kirby, on the other hand, was short and round like a barrel. Instead of smiling, he was always chomping on a cigar. About the only thing they had in common, aside from comic books, was where and how they grew up. Like Iron Man, Jack and Stan were born in New York City. Unlike the millionaire Tony Stark, however, both Stan and Jack grew up poor while their immigrant parents struggled to find work.

THE BRICK WALL

Stan Lee was born on December 28, 1922, and was raised on the Upper West Side of Manhattan. His parents came to America from Romania, hoping to escape religious and economic struggles.

As a child, Stan had one love, along with one motivation. His love was reading. He read everything from the labels on ketchup bottles to Shakespeare. He read so much that his mom made a stand to hold his books so he could read while he ate at the dinner table.

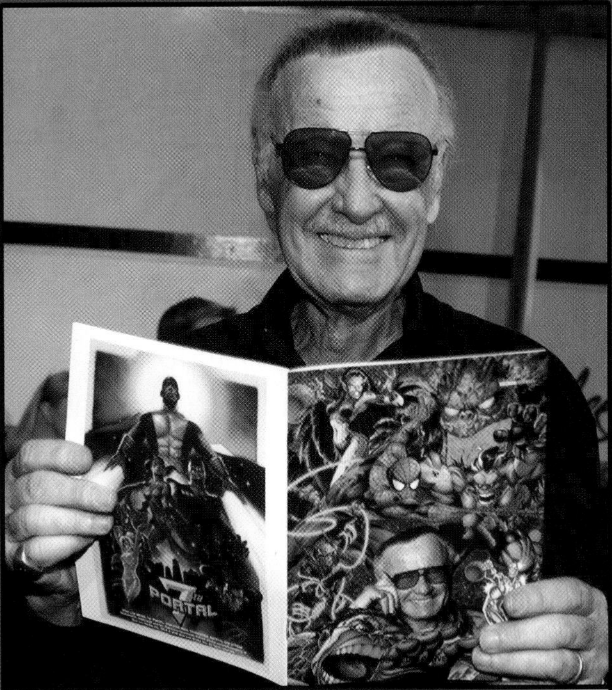
PORTAL
Stan Lee has become almost as recognizable in the comic book industry as some of his famous characters, like the Incredible Hulk and Spider-Man. These characters have also often appeared in films, television shows, and even video games.

His motivation came from the view of a brick wall outside the family's apartment. The view depressed him and he could never hear whether other children were outside playing. He wanted to be a success so that someday he could afford the kind of view that offered something besides bricks and a dirty alley.

Stan's other interests at a young age were watching movies, riding his bike, and writing. All of these activities allowed him to enter his imagination and escape the poverty that his family faced.

When he was just seventeen years old, after working as a drugstore delivery boy and an usher in a movie theater, he went to work for his cousin-in-law Martin Goodman. It was 1940, and Martin

Goodman's company, Timely Publications (which would later be called Atlas and then Marvel), was just starting to get into the comic book business with a new Super Hero named Captain America.

At first, Stan played only a minor role in the company. He swept the floor, fetched sandwiches, and refilled ink for the artists, including Jack Kirby himself. But Stan was ambitious, and within a few months, he was working on his first story for *Captain America Comics*. Within the year, he was contributing more creative work. Soon he climbed his way up to an editor position, in charge of the other writers and artists. It was a job he would keep for the next thirty years. To this day, Stan Lee is still directly involved with the production of Marvel products.

ALL HAIL THE KING

Jack Kirby's nickname among fans and fellow artists alike was "the King," and it is a title he well deserved. No other artist in the history of

ANTI-SEMITISM

"Stan Lee" and "Jack Kirby" are not the artists' birth names. Stan Lee was born Stanley Martin Lieber, and Jack Kirby's name was Jacob Kurtzberg. Both were from Jewish families. In the early 1900s, it was common for people of Jewish heritage to change their names in order to avoid anti-Semitism, a prejudicial attitude toward Jewish people. Both have acknowledged that anti-Semitism was common during their careers, but neither claims to have changed his name as a direct result.

comics worked on so many different characters, drew more artwork, or had a style as influential as that of Jack Kirby.

Jack was born on August 28, 1917, on the Lower East Side, which was a poor, dangerous immigrant neighborhood in New York City. If Stan's motivation to escape poverty was the brick wall outside his apartment, Jack's was more like the bricks being thrown at his head. Violence ruled everything around him. There were fights at school, fights outside his front door,

Jack Kirby, pictured here in 1947, was known as a tireless worker throughout his career, especially when creating an original story. He would often stay up until three or four A.M., sleep for a few hours, and then head straight back to his inks and pencils.

and fights among the local gangs that terrorized the streets. The action that Kirby brought to the pages of the comics he drew, including the detailed depictions of punches, kicks, and elbow jabs, surely had its origins in his own early experiences.

When Jack was growing up, there weren't any comic book stores or even many comic books. Most of the books were reprints of comic strips from the newspaper. The action and the artwork stirred something in him nonetheless, and he dreamed of going to art school to learn how to create his own work for the newspapers. Unfortunately, however, there was no money to be had for a higher education, so he went to work instead.

As it turned out, Jack didn't need art school—he had natural talent. One of his first jobs was working on the animated television cartoon *Popeye*. His ability to draw realistic and exciting characters soon propelled him into the comic book business. By the time he was twenty-one, he was working full-time as an artist, making about $15 a week. This wasn't a lot of money for the time, but for someone as poor as Jack, it seemed like a decent wage.

In 1940, when he was twenty-three years old, he went to work for Timely Publications and co-created *Captain America*, the first comic popular enough to compete with *Superman* and *Batman*. The first issue sold over a million copies and made Jack Kirby one of the most sought-after artists in the business. It was a reputation he would maintain until his death on February 6, 1994, at the age of seventy-six.

2 DIFFERENT HEROES FOR A DIFFERENT GENERATION

It's hard to believe now, but there was a time when Super Heroes like Iron Man weren't very popular. By the late 1950s, characters who wore disguises and could fly or crush tanks with their bare hands weren't selling many comics. For Kirby and Lee, the *Captain America* comics they worked on together in the 1940s had been the high point of their careers.

World War II in particular was a boost for the series because the real-world villains of Adolf Hitler and the Nazis provided the perfect bad guys for Captain America to squash. As the war came to an end, however, so did the popularity of this type of hero.

After enthusiasm for *Captain America* died out and it was no longer published, things got even worse for the comic book industry. Since superhero titles weren't selling, publishers switched to other genres, or categories, like romance, crime, and westerns.

These comic genres were popular, but that popularity came at a price. Much like today's criticism toward TV and video games, many people thought comics were corrupting children. They blamed bad behavior, poor grades, and even criminal activities on comic books. As a result, the entire industry suffered, and by the end of the 1950s, it was near collapse.

Only *Superman* and *Batman*, published by DC (Detective Comics), were popular enough to survive the darkest days of the comic book business. The plots had become recycled, however, and the artwork lacked the creative punch needed to thrill the readers. If a Super Hero comic was going to be exciting and sell thousands of issues, it was going to have to be different from what DC was offering.

SUPERPOWERS AND SUPER FLAWS

By 1961, after years spent working through the comic book industry's decline, Stan Lee and Jack Kirby were ready to quit. Both were frustrated by the lack of interest in superheroes and the poor sales of comic books in general, but they decided to give it one last try. They had no idea that they were about to produce some of the most creative and popular comic books of all time.

Their first hit in November 1961 was *The Fantastic Four*, a comic that featured a group of people who, upon being exposed to high levels of a mysterious, green cosmic ray, develop special powers. On the surface, *The Fantastic Four* sounds like a hundred other comic books that littered the newsstand racks over the previous thirty years, but there was something different about these characters.

In addition to Jack Kirby's art, which seemed to jump off the pages, the Fantastic Four spent a lot of time arguing, something most comic book characters had never done before. Their disagreements weren't with criminals, demons, or other superpowered villains, but each other. They dressed, talked, and acted a lot like regular people. Readers identified with them, and fans responded by buying up the issues and writing letters to Marvel that voiced their approval.

WORLD, MEET IRON MAN

Kirby and Lee were quick to follow up the success of *The Fantastic Four* with a slew of new comics with characters that offered readers Super Heroes whose personal lives were as interesting as their amazing abilities. When Iron Man joined the Marvel family in 1963, fans

THE MARVEL METHOD

Collaborating on a comic book as a group was a new way of working at the time, and is referred to by comic book historians as the Marvel Method. Although the Marvel Method produced new and exciting comics, it also led to controversy. Due to the popularity of the Marvel characters created during this time period, the person who claimed to have come up with the ideas could become extremely rich. For many years, Stan Lee was the most successful at convincing the public that he was the originator behind the Marvel Universe. Only after a careful examination of the art and a number of lawsuits has a closer version of the truth been revealed. Nowadays, most people accept that the characters found in the early Marvel comics were indeed the result of a group effort.

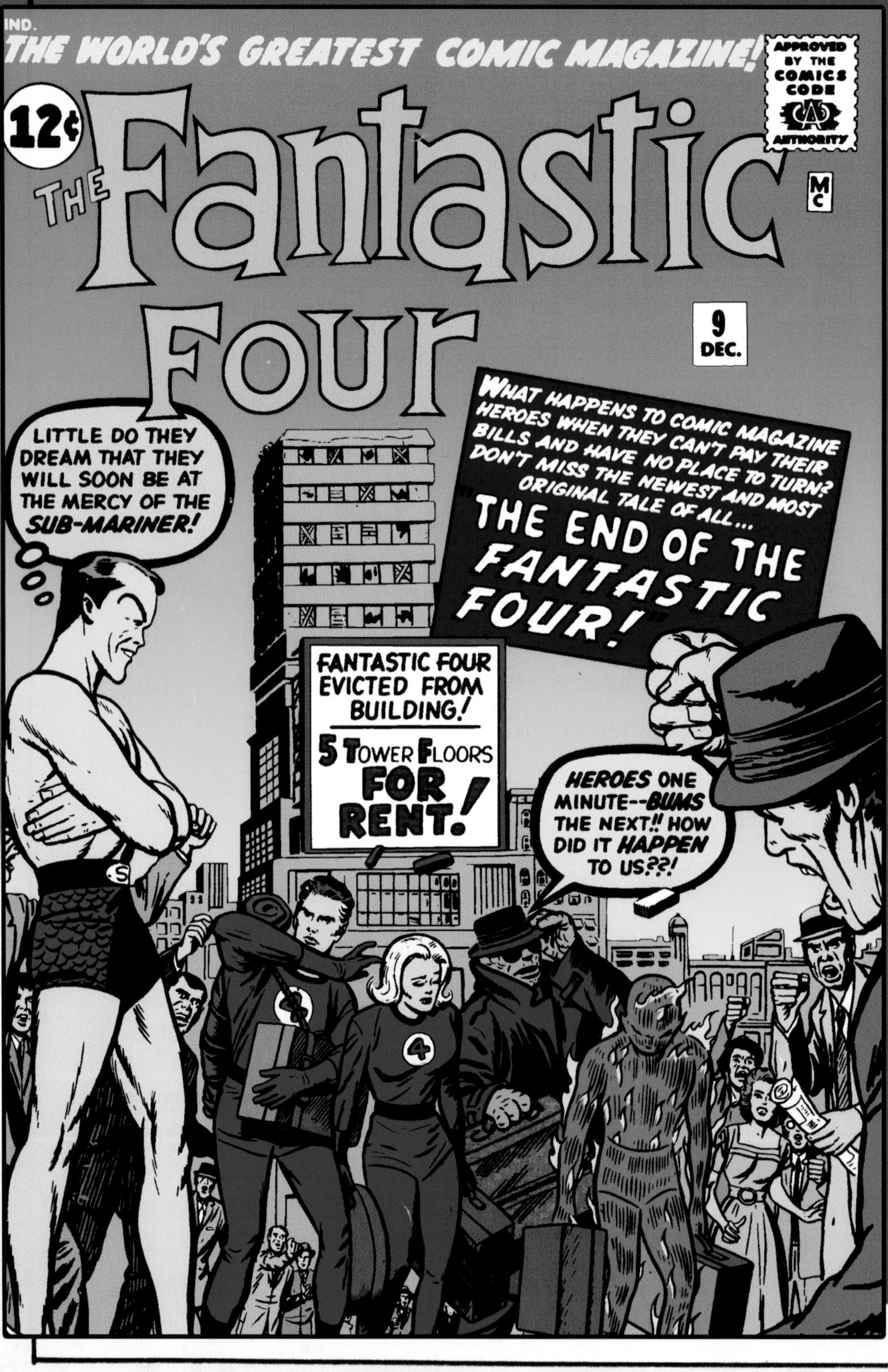
IND.
THE WORLD'S GREATEST COMIC MAGAZINE!
APPROVED BY THE COMICS CODE AUTHORITY
12¢
THE Fantastic FOUR
MC
9 DEC.
LITTLE DO THEY DREAM THAT THEY WILL SOON BE AT THE MERCY OF THE SUB-MARINER!
WHAT HAPPENS TO COMIC MAGAZINE HEROES WHEN THEY CAN'T PAY THEIR BILLS AND HAVE NO PLACE TO TURN? DON'T MISS THE NEWEST AND MOST ORIGINAL TALE OF ALL... "THE END OF THE FANTASTIC FOUR!"
FANTASTIC FOUR EVICTED FROM BUILDING!
5 TOWER FLOORS FOR RENT!
HEROES ONE MINUTE--BUMS THE NEXT!! HOW DID IT HAPPEN TO US??!

were introduced to a character who had problems in his love life, with his business, and, in later issues, with politics and alcohol.

Most of the Super Heroes from previous generations were either born with their powers or acquired them in order to bring more peace and tranquility to the world. Neither of these scenarios applied to Tony Stark. He became Iron Man out of a need for survival. Although he was heroic and did his fair share of saving the world, Stark was also motivated by self-interest, such as protecting his weapons-manufacturing business. He was a Super Hero, but to fans, he also came across as a real person.

OUT OF THE BOX

Iron Man and the other Marvel comics also stood out because of the freedom Stan Lee allowed the artists who worked for him. Most publishers before Marvel were very rigid in their production techniques. The writers would give the artists a page-by-page breakdown of text that included what would be drawn in each of the panels (the boxes that are filled in with drawings and can be manipulated to affect the pace of a story). This gave the artists very little choice in how to visually portray the action or how many panels they could use.

The Fantastic Four was Lee and Kirby's first attempt at breaking from traditional Super Hero characters. These heroes were so different that in the first few issues they even wore regular clothes instead of the familiar blue suits that would become their trademark outfits. This cover (left), from the early years of the series, shows the team facing one of the most realistic aspects of living in New York City: high rents.

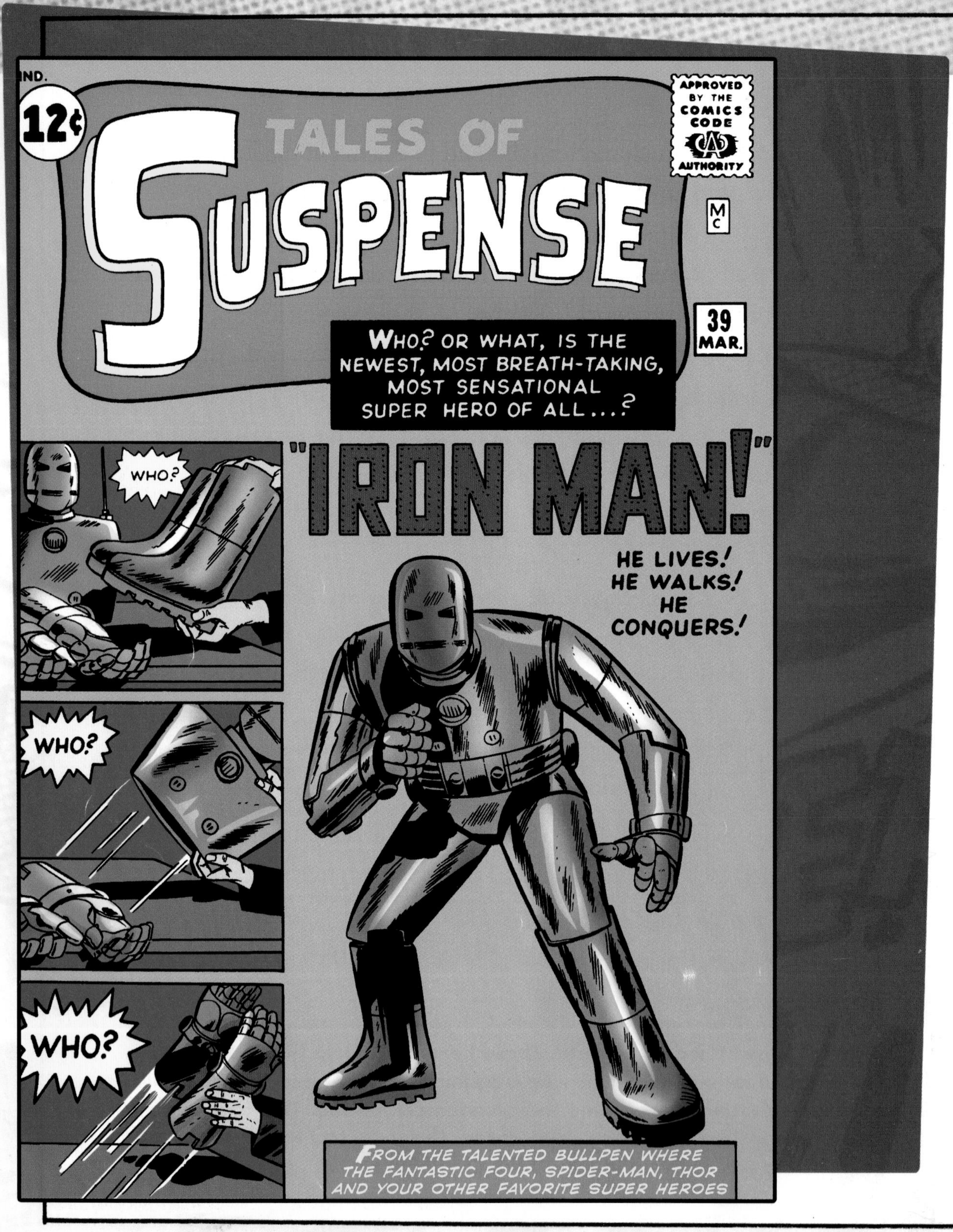
IND.
12¢
TALES OF SUSPENSE
APPROVED BY THE COMICS CODE AUTHORITY
MC
39 MAR.
WHO? OR WHAT, IS THE NEWEST, MOST BREATH-TAKING, MOST SENSATIONAL SUPER HERO OF ALL...?
"IRON MAN!"
WHO?
WHO?
WHO?
HE LIVES! HE WALKS! HE CONQUERS!
FROM THE TALENTED BULLPEN WHERE THE FANTASTIC FOUR, SPIDER-MAN, THOR AND YOUR OTHER FAVORITE SUPER HEROES

Lee, because he was so busy writing the dialogue and trying to come up with new ideas along with the other artists who worked for him, didn't have the time to make these detailed outlines. Therefore, Kirby and others who had natural storytelling ability with images instead of words were able to produce some of the best work of their careers.

The multiple co-creators for each story allowed for significant collaboration among the Marvel staff to come up with new characters and plotlines. Sometimes, Lee would have an idea for a new character and then Kirby or another artist would add his own thoughts while drawing the story. Then after the story was completed, Lee would go back and either add dialogue or edit the dialogue that the artist had provided. The result was comics that had better art, better action, and more style than their competitors.

Jack Kirby's cover art, left, for *Tales of Suspense* #39 set the tone and style for future *Iron Man* artists. This issue also included the stories "The Last Rocket" and "Gundar," but fans were drawn to Iron Man, who was clearly the comic's star. The gray-colored armor seen here lasted for a single issue. Stark changed it to gold in *Tales of Suspense* #40 because of a comment made by one of his girlfriends.

3 THE MAN IN THE METAL SUIT

Comic fans were first introduced to Iron Man in March 1963. At the time, Marvel was still called Atlas, and although its Super Hero titles like *The Fantastic Four* were beginning to pick up in sales, it was still publishing a variety of other types of comic books. One of these was a series about monsters called *Tales of Suspense*, which featured a different story each month. In issue #39, Lee and Kirby introduced Iron Man, and he immediately became the star of the series. He was so popular that they changed the title to *Tales of Suspense Featuring the Power of Iron Man*.

The original Iron Man in *Tales of Suspense* resembled a large gray robot that would not look out of place in a 1950s' science fiction film about space aliens. He was slow-moving and bulky, almost like a metallic Frankenstein. In his next appearance, his armor went from gray to gold. Soon it would become more sleek and aerodynamic, and Stark would be able to fold it up and fit it inside a briefcase in case Iron Man was needed.

IRON MAN IS BORN

The first Iron Man story follows Stark as he goes to Vietnam to test one of his new weapons for the United States military. While in the jungle, an explosion hurts Stark and damages his heart. A villainous warlord named Wong Chu then captures him and discovers that Stark is one of the world's most famous weapons designers.

Chu demands that Stark build him a weapon. Stark agrees, but instead of building a device that would be used against the United States, he has an idea. With the help of a fellow prisoner, a scientist named Professor Yinsen, Stark builds a powerful iron suit. The suit can fly and uses magnetic force to control metal objects. It also has the ability to keep Stark's heart beating. However, it needs an electrical charge, like from a battery, to work.

Professor Yinsen distracts their captors long enough to allow the suit to charge, but he is killed before Stark can save him. Stark has trouble at first getting used to his new armored suit, but he quickly adapts to its weight and strength and easily defeats Wong Chu. Although he has saved himself, he must always wear the metal chest plate to keep his heart beating. Additionally, he must make sure there is enough power to keep it functioning. From this point on he is Iron Man—an identity he keeps secret by pretending

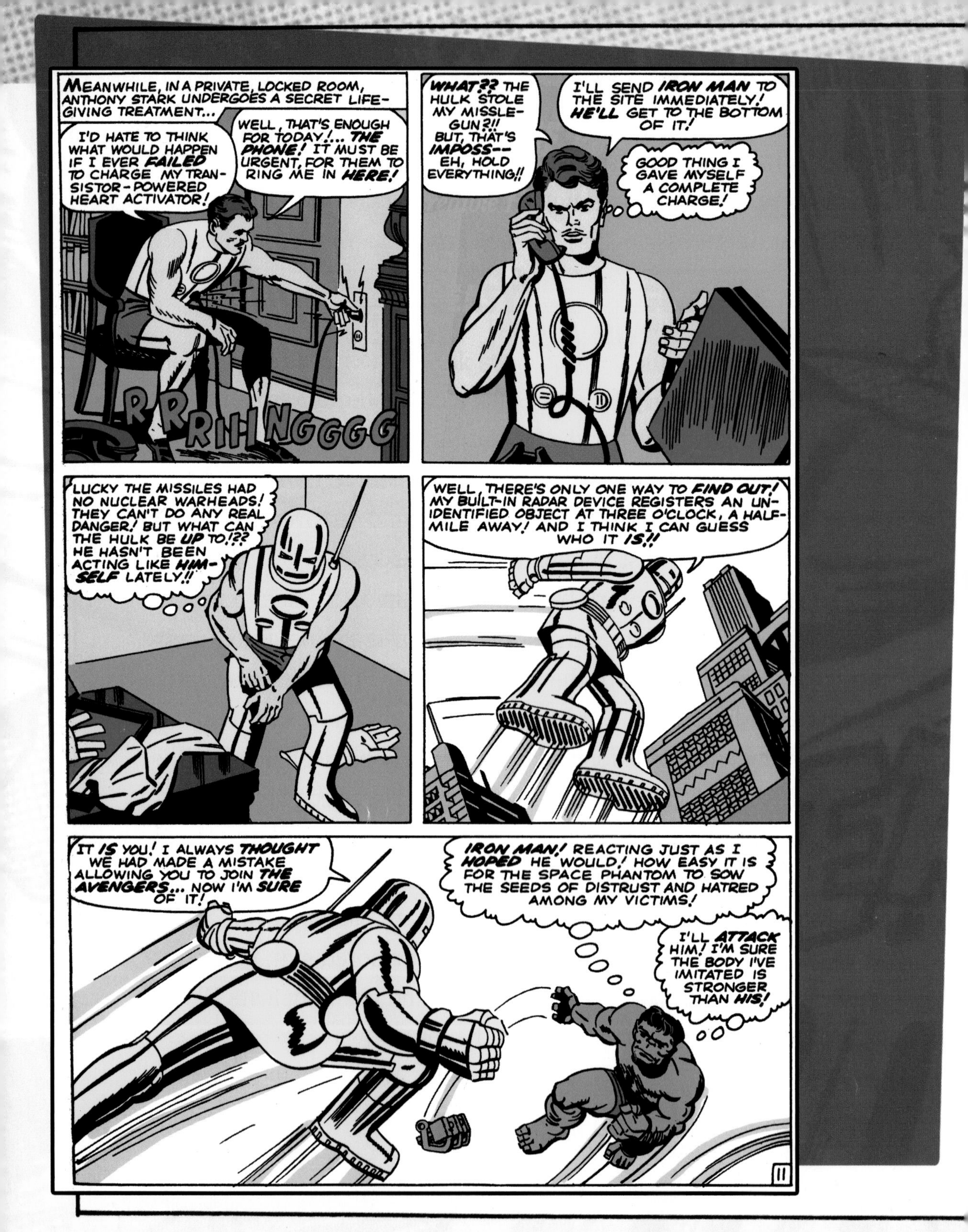
MEANWHILE, IN A PRIVATE, LOCKED ROOM, ANTHONY STARK UNDERGOES A SECRET LIFE-GIVING TREATMENT...
I'D HATE TO THINK WHAT WOULD HAPPEN IF I EVER FAILED TO CHARGE MY TRANSISTOR-POWERED HEART ACTIVATOR!
WELL, THAT'S ENOUGH FOR TODAY!... THE PHONE! IT MUST BE URGENT, FOR THEM TO RING ME IN HERE!
RRRIIINGGGG
WHAT?? THE HULK STOLE MY MISSLE-GUN?!! BUT, THAT'S IMPOSS-- EH, HOLD EVERYTHING!!
I'LL SEND IRON MAN TO THE SITE IMMEDIATELY! HE'LL GET TO THE BOTTOM OF IT!
GOOD THING I GAVE MYSELF A COMPLETE CHARGE!
LUCKY THE MISSILES HAD NO NUCLEAR WARHEADS! THEY CAN'T DO ANY REAL DANGER! BUT WHAT CAN THE HULK BE UP TO!?? HE HASN'T BEEN ACTING LIKE HIMSELF LATELY!!
WELL, THERE'S ONLY ONE WAY TO FIND OUT! MY BUILT-IN RADAR DEVICE REGISTERS AN UNIDENTIFIED OBJECT AT THREE O'CLOCK, A HALF-MILE AWAY! AND I THINK I CAN GUESS WHO IT IS!!
IT IS YOU! I ALWAYS THOUGHT WE HAD MADE A MISTAKE ALLOWING YOU TO JOIN THE AVENGERS... NOW I'M SURE OF IT!
IRON MAN! REACTING JUST AS I HOPED HE WOULD! HOW EASY IT IS FOR THE SPACE PHANTOM TO SOW THE SEEDS OF DISTRUST AND HATRED AMONG MY VICTIMS!
I'LL ATTACK HIM! I'M SURE THE BODY I'VE IMITATED IS STRONGER THAN HIS!

that the man in the metal suit is Tony Stark's personal bodyguard rather than himself.

TONY STARK, BEHIND THE MASK

In Iron Man's early days, Tony Stark was suave and sophisticated. He was a rich gentleman who had a different girlfriend in every city. He seemed more like a handsome Hollywood celebrity or a star athlete than the scientific genius that he was. Stark was also extremely patriotic, more so than almost any comic book character aside from Captain America. He was devoted to developing weapons and gadgets that would aid America against foreign enemies.

Like any Marvel character with a long history, dramatic changes have occurred to both Iron Man and his secret identity, Tony Stark. A number of different artists and writers have worked on the comic over the years, and they have each brought their own unique ideas and visions to the character. As drastic as some of these interpretations may be, the original concept as envisioned by Kirby, Lee, and Don Heck (another co-creator) still provides the basis for most of the modern Iron Man adventures.

This page (left) from an Iron Man comic shows a typical day for Stark. He charges himself in a wall socket, puts on his armor, and then battles the Incredible Hulk. Stark would eventually have a heart transplant to let him live his life without the iron chest plate. Dealing with problems like stolen weapons or misunderstandings with other heroes, however, would never go away.

THE INVINCIBLE
IRON MAN
MARVEL COMICS GROUP
12¢ IND.
1 MAY
MCG
APPROVED BY THE COMICS CODE AUTHORITY
BIG PREMIERE ISSUE

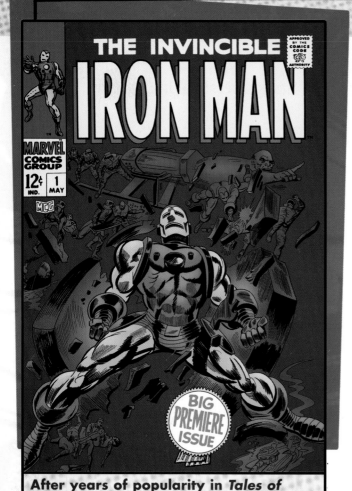

After years of popularity in *Tales of Suspense* and an appearance with the Sub-Mariner that lasted only one issue, Iron Man was finally given his own comic *(above)*. It became one of Marvel's all-time hits.

THROUGH THE YEARS

In 1968, after thrilling fans for years in the pages of *Tales of Suspense*, "Shell Head" was given his own comic book series called *The Invincible Iron Man*. The first ten years or so of the series continued the narrative established in *Tales of Suspense*. Many of Iron Man's arch villains, including the Mandarin, the Crimson Dynamo, and the Melter, all made appearances during this time. In this era, Iron Man became the first hero to battle the cosmic villain Thanos, who in time would prove to become one of the Marvel Universe's most menacing threats. The struggle for control of Stark's company, Stark International, was also introduced. His business rivals such as Roxxon Oil, Justin Hammer, and Obadiah Stane all wanted the company and the weapons it produced. The drama of who would control it would become a long-running theme throughout the rest of *Iron Man*'s history.

The late 1970s and early 1980s were a period of significant growth and change for Iron Man. While the original character from the 1960s appeared more human than the contemporary heroes of the day, starting in 1978, *Iron Man* took this even further. In these issues, Stark would face something worse than the Melter's rays and even more realistic than most Marvel fans had come to expect. Tony Stark became an alcoholic.

Stark's drinking problem, like his difficulty in keeping control of Stark International or defeating the Mandarin, would exist for many years. Sometimes, he would be so ill that somebody else would have to take on the responsibility of becoming Iron Man. This duty usually fell upon Stark's best friend and personal pilot, Jim Rhodes. Rhodes wore the metal armor on many occasions when Stark could not,

HELPFUL HANDS

Jack Kirby and Stan Lee developed the idea for Iron Man's first appearance, but there was another important artist involved. Don Heck, who was a Marvel artist, is also credited as being a co-creator. He took Lee and Kirby's ideas and sketches, and contributed the bulk of the finished artwork and basic plot structure for the series' early, formative years. He worked on the series again in the 1970s. *Tales of Suspense* #39 also credits Larry Lieber, Stan's younger brother, as the scriptwriter, which means he wrote the plot and the dialogue. Many other artists, including *Spider-Man's* co-creator, Steve Ditko, have worked on *Iron Man*. As the success of the comic continued, some of Marvel's best writers and creative talents contributed to the story, including David Michelinie, who introduced a number of *Iron Man's* more complex stories, and John Byrne, who was one of Marvel's most respected artists in the late 1980s.

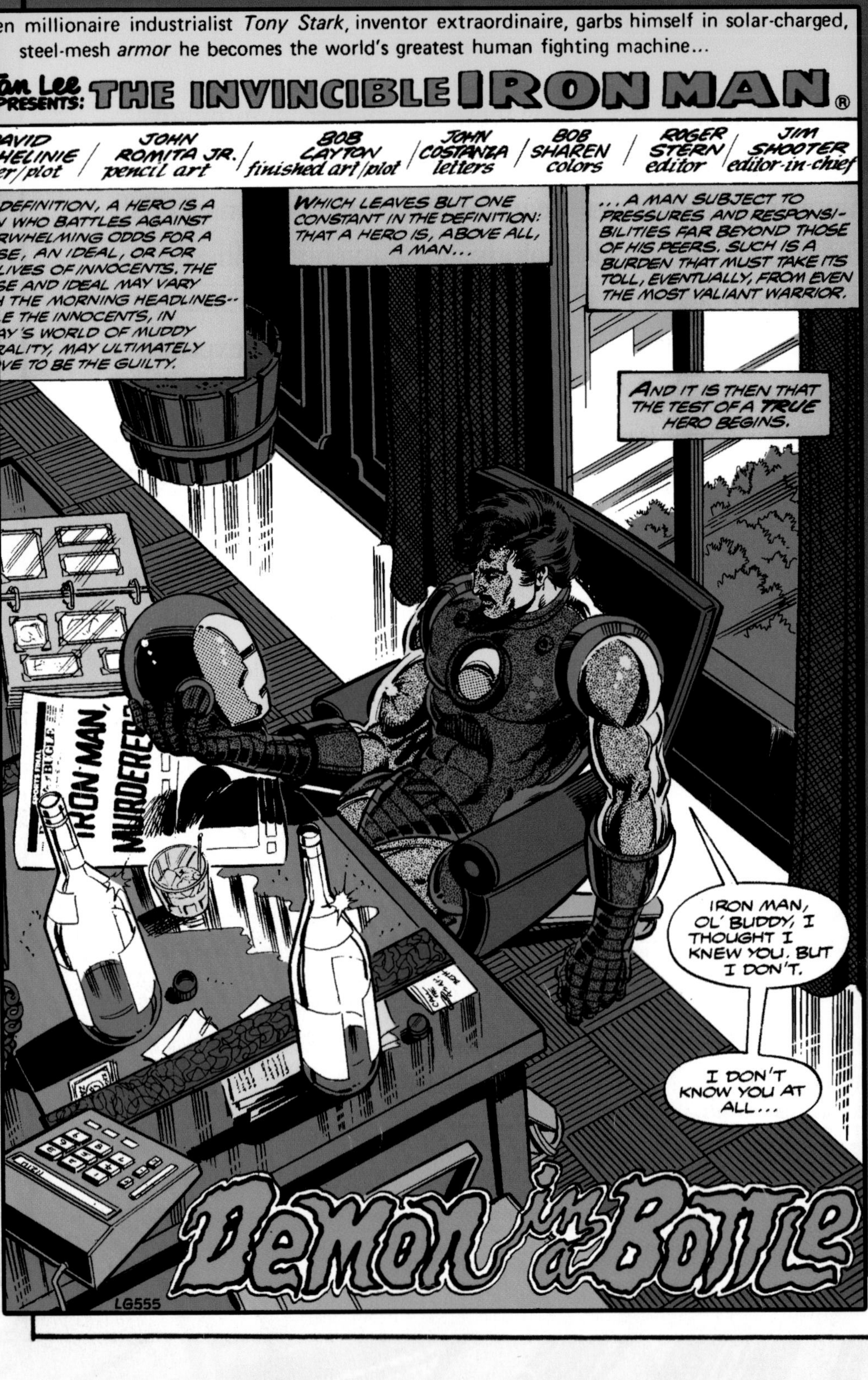
en millionaire industrialist Tony Stark, inventor extraordinaire, garbs himself in solar-charged, steel-mesh armor he becomes the world's greatest human fighting machine...
an Lee PRESENTS: THE INVINCIBLE IRON MAN®
AVID HELINIE er/plot
JOHN ROMITA JR. pencil art
BOB LAYTON finished art/plot
JOHN COSTANZA letters
BOB SHAREN colors
ROGER STERN editor
JIM SHOOTER editor-in-chief
DEFINITION, A HERO IS A N WHO BATTLES AGAINST RWHELMING ODDS FOR A SE, AN IDEAL, OR FOR LIVES OF INNOCENTS. THE SE AND IDEAL MAY VARY H THE MORNING HEADLINES-- E THE INNOCENTS, IN AY'S WORLD OF MUDDY RALITY, MAY ULTIMATELY VE TO BE THE GUILTY.
WHICH LEAVES BUT ONE CONSTANT IN THE DEFINITION: THAT A HERO IS, ABOVE ALL, A MAN...
...A MAN SUBJECT TO PRESSURES AND RESPONSIBILITIES FAR BEYOND THOSE OF HIS PEERS. SUCH IS A BURDEN THAT MUST TAKE ITS TOLL, EVENTUALLY, FROM EVEN THE MOST VALIANT WARRIOR.
AND IT IS THEN THAT THE TEST OF A TRUE HERO BEGINS.
BUGLE
IRON MAN, MURDERER
IRON MAN, OL' BUDDY, I THOUGHT I KNEW YOU. BUT I DON'T.
I DON'T KNOW YOU AT ALL...
DEMON in a BOTTLE
LG555

including during the legendary series *Marvel Super Heroes Secret Wars*. Stark later gave Rhodes his own unique suit of armor, making him War Machine, a Super Hero in his own right. It was also thanks to Rhodes and his friendship that Stark would eventually overcome alcoholism and continue on as Iron Man.

As if alcohol weren't a big enough problem, Iron Man would have another personal demon to face. In the *Invincible Iron Man* stories from the late 1980s, Tony Stark is determined to destroy all of his inventions that have been used to hurt people. This quest puts him up against not only the criminals who have stolen his designs but also the United States government and some of his fellow Super Heroes. Any weapon he had built that could be used for war Stark wanted destroyed, even if it was in the hands of his allies. This threatened his role as a Super Hero somewhat since the public came to see Iron Man as more of an enemy than an ally.

THE END OF AN ERA

It wouldn't be alcohol or the attempted hostile takeovers of Stark International that would be the ultimate downfall of *The Invincible Iron Man*, but another period of poor comic sales. After 34 years and

Despite all the fantastical and supernatural plotlines in *Iron Man*, what distinguished it the most from other comics was Tony Stark's battle with alcoholism (left, in a 1979 splash page). It was somewhat risky for Marvel to have a character with such a serious flaw, but it made Iron Man one of the most humanized Super Heroes in comics history. Fan reaction was generally positive.

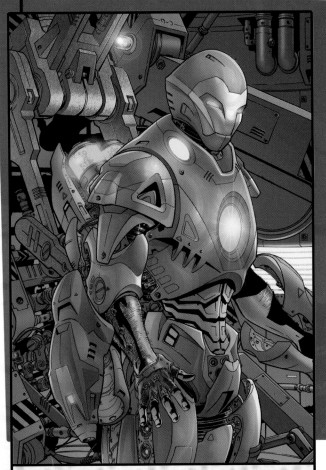

In the *Ultimate Iron Man* series, shown here, writers put aside everything that came before and started an entirely new comic inspired by the original ideas from the 1960s. While an armored suit and problems with alcohol were still central to the series, almost everything else was changed, including Iron Man's origin and powers.

332 issues, the last *Invincible Iron Man* appeared on store shelves in September 1996.

Although this marked the end of an era for one of Marvel's longest-running series, it also ushered in a new life for both Iron Man and many of his colleagues, such as Captain America and the Fantastic Four. In the years that have followed the last issue, Iron Man has been reconceived in a number of different series, including *Heroes Reborn*, *Bad Blood*, *Heroes Return*, and *Ultimate Iron Man*. Some take place in other worlds or other time periods. In some instances, Iron Man is a Super Villain instead of a hero. Some of these comics have stayed true to the original vision, while others have taken an entirely new direction. Either way, the character of Iron Man continues to change and be introduced to new generations of Marvel fans.

4 IRON FANS

A comic book's popularity relies on more than just interesting stories and great artwork. A character needs to have something special in order to make him or her stand out. *Iron Man*'s continued success over the years was the result of the style and content established by Kirby and Lee. Even though they had a number of hits before *Iron Man*, they still brought something new to the series, and especially to the character of Tony Stark.

MIXING IT UP

Before Marvel became successful, comic publishers released a variety of series in different categories or genres. There were comics about cowboys, war, and detectives. Any topic that had action or drama was translated into comic books.

29

For the most part, superheroes had their own genre. What made Iron Man different, and what Lee and Kirby tried to do with many of their heroes, was combine the genres. Out of all the comic books Marvel published in those formative years of the early 1960s, *Iron Man* is perhaps the best example of multiple genres in one book. Although Iron Man is above all else a Super Hero, both the original *Tales of Suspense* and *The Invincible Iron Man* combined elements of war, romance, and espionage (spying) into the storylines.

It is surprising that out of all these genres, romance was the one that played an ongoing role in Tony Stark's personal life. Including stories about Stark while he wasn't Iron Man contributed appeal to a wider and often older audience. College students in particular responded to this storyline topic. Unlike other Super Heroes, who always fought one type of villain or were drawn in the same style panel after panel, Iron Man was a lot more varied and unpredictable.

WHO DOES THIS GUY THINK HE IS?

While Jack Kirby was a drawing master, Stan Lee had a flare for dialogue and unusual character development. Sometimes this meant that a co-created hero would be a bit strange or troubled. Lee wanted to give audiences something different so that they would keep buying issue after issue.

Tony Stark was distinct, not just because of the problems he would come to face, but because he offered readers a new type of secret identity. There were other millionaires with public personas who became crime-fighting avengers, but Stark was not like them. On the surface, he was what many would consider to be an unsympathetic type. He was a patriotic industrialist who made his money by developing weapons to be used in war. He was proud of his career and was interested in making money and living a life of luxury. Later, other writers would have Stark question these qualities and feel both guilt and regret about his chosen business, but at the beginning Stark was content with his position in the world. This made Stark appealing to a comic book audience who would probably hate him in real life but enjoyed reading about him because he wasn't the type of character found in any other comic.

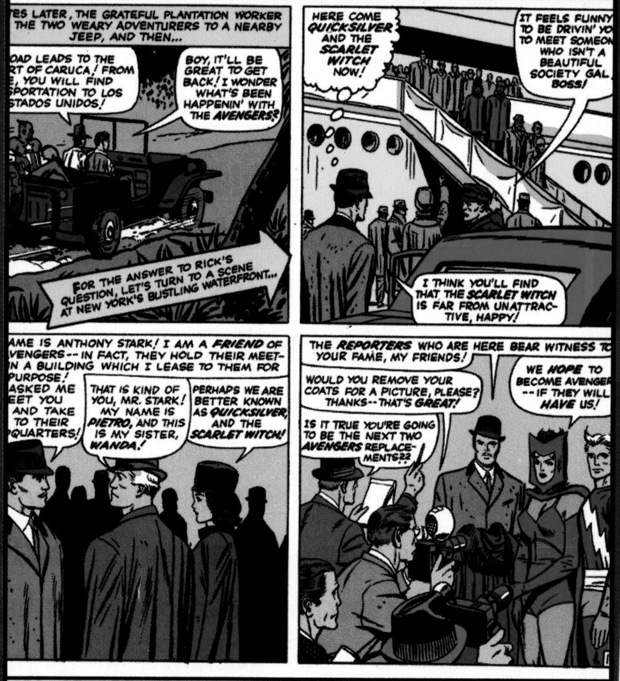

ES LATER, THE GRATEFUL PLANTATION WORKER THE TWO WEARY ADVENTURERS TO A NEARBY JEEP, AND THEN...
OAD LEADS TO THE RT OF CARUCA! FROM E, YOU WILL FIND SPORTATION TO LOS STADOS UNIDOS!
BOY, IT'LL BE GREAT TO GET BACK! I WONDER WHAT'S BEEN HAPPENIN' WITH THE AVENGERS?
FOR THE ANSWER TO RICK'S QUESTION, LET'S TURN TO A SCENE AT NEW YORK'S BUSTLING WATERFRONT...
HERE COME QUICKSILVER AND THE SCARLET WITCH NOW!
IT FEELS FUNNY TO BE DRIVIN' YO TO MEET SOMEON WHO ISN'T A BEAUTIFUL SOCIETY GAL, BOSS!
I THINK YOU'LL FIND THAT THE SCARLET WITCH IS FAR FROM UNATTRACTIVE, HAPPY!
AME IS ANTHONY STARK! I AM A FRIEND OF VENGERS-- IN FACT, THEY HOLD THEIR MEET- N A BUILDING WHICH I LEASE TO THEM FOR PURPOSE!
ASKED ME EET YOU AND TAKE TO THEIR QUARTERS!
THAT IS KIND OF YOU, MR. STARK! MY NAME IS PIETRO, AND THIS IS MY SISTER, WANDA!
PERHAPS WE ARE BETTER KNOWN AS QUICKSILVER, AND THE SCARLET WITCH!
THE REPORTERS WHO ARE HERE BEAR WITNESS TO YOUR FAME, MY FRIENDS!
WOULD YOU REMOVE YOUR COATS FOR A PICTURE, PLEASE? THANKS--THAT'S GREAT!
IS IT TRUE YOU'RE GOING TO BE THE NEXT TWO AVENGERS REPLACEMENTS??
WE HOPE TO BECOME AVENGER --IF THEY WILL HAVE US!

Since the beginning, Tony Stark has always been seen as a ladies' man. However, most of his relationships were short-lived or ended badly for him.

Lee also made *The Invincible Iron Man* and many of the other Marvel titles stand out by including humorous comments in the text boxes that often referenced the artists and writers. For example, instead of saying "Written by Stan Lee," he would say, "Scribbled and Scrawled by Stan Lee" or "Story by Stan Lee, Idol of Millions." He often used this type of language, writing things like, "The monstrous menace of the mind-staggering Titanium Man!" The technique gave readers the sense that Lee was talking directly to them. At the same time, it acknowledged that the stories and situations were sometimes silly or overly dramatic. For older audiences, such as college students, it was like being part of an inside joke. It made them feel connected to the comic. A fan of *Tales of Suspense*, for example, knew the names of all the different artists and writers who worked on its production because of the funny nicknames Lee gave to his staff in the credits. It was another way to reach out to an audience who appreciated humor and understood that comic book writers and artists didn't necessarily take themselves too seriously.

A CHILL IN THE AIR

Although comic books are usually works of pure fiction, the Marvel writers liked to use real-world events to increase readership. In the 1940s, World War II generated a huge interest in comics like *Captain America*. They allowed readers the chance to escape reality and also watch war enemies be defeated on the comics' pages.

When *The Invincible Iron Man* was first published, World War II had been over for almost twenty years, and writers like Stan Lee needed new enemies to use as villains. They didn't have to look far: newspapers were filled with fears and questions about the Soviet Union, a former ally of the United States.

Many American citizens were afraid of the Soviet Union because they thought the Soviets wanted to dominate the world with their political ideas. Although America and the Soviet Union never directly fought each other on the battlefield, the tension between the two countries led to war in other countries, such as Vietnam and Korea. The conflict with the Soviet Union, which started at the end of World War II and lasted through the early 1990s, was called the Cold War.

Since the Cold War caused so much fear and tension among Americans, many of Iron Man's earliest enemies were associated with the Soviet Union and its largest ally, China. These villains included the Crimson Dynamo, a robot created by an evil Russian scientist named Professor Vanko. The Mandarin, who gained his powers from the ten rings he wore, was the secret leader behind the Chinese army. The Black Widow was a Russian spy, and Titanium Man was built by the Russian government to try to

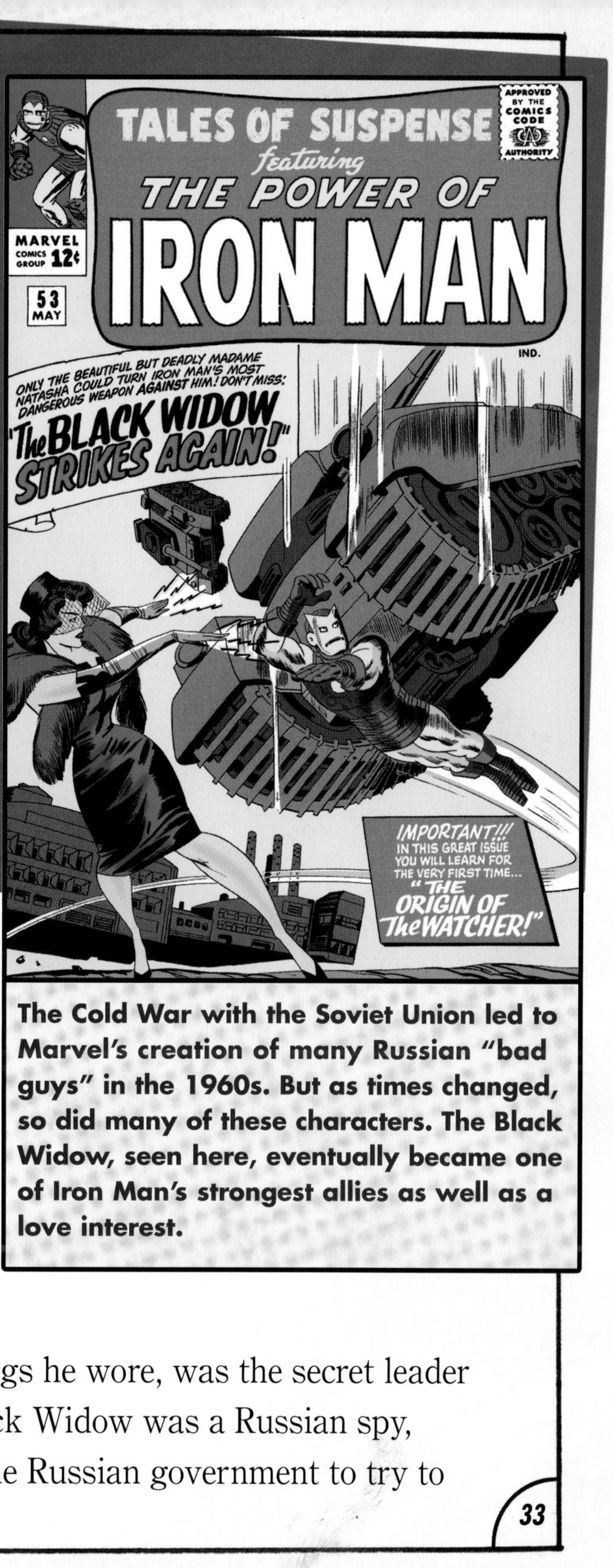
TALES OF SUSPENSE
featuring
THE POWER OF
IRON MAN
APPROVED BY THE COMICS CODE AUTHORITY
MARVEL COMICS GROUP 12¢
53 MAY
IND.
ONLY THE BEAUTIFUL BUT DEADLY MADAME NATASHA COULD TURN IRON MAN'S MOST DANGEROUS WEAPON AGAINST HIM! DON'T MISS:
"The BLACK WIDOW STRIKES AGAIN!"
IMPORTANT!!! IN THIS GREAT ISSUE YOU WILL LEARN FOR THE VERY FIRST TIME... "THE ORIGIN OF The WATCHER!"

The Cold War with the Soviet Union led to Marvel's creation of many Russian "bad guys" in the 1960s. But as times changed, so did many of these characters. The Black Widow, seen here, eventually became one of Iron Man's strongest allies as well as a love interest.

THE AVENGERS

As an editor, Stan Lee liked to have characters from one Marvel comic cross over into another, or have different characters team up for an entirely new series. One of the most popular team-ups in comic book history is the Avengers, which originally included Iron Man, the Mighty Thor, the Incredible Hulk, Ant Man, and the Wasp. Although this combination would change many times throughout Marvel's history, Iron Man has always been associated with the team and was their first leader until Captain America took the job in issue #4. As Tony Stark, he also funded the Avengers' expenses through a nonprofit organization named after his mother, and let them use his mansion as their headquarters.

With the popularity of Marvel's characters snowballing in the early 1960s, Stan Lee thought that instead of having only one hero per issue, why not have some of the most successful heroes appear together in one comic? Thus the Avengers were born. In keeping with Marvel style, they spent as much time bickering as they did stomping the bad guys.

match Iron Man's armor. Even Iron Man's original enemy, Wong Chu, was associated with Russia and China.

Looking at these early enemies, many would consider that the Cold War characters Iron Man fought are negative stereotypes of Russian and Chinese people. A stereotype is an oversimplified idea of a person and is often associated with prejudice and racism. Many writers, not only of comic books, use stereotypes as an easy way to describe a character. For example, a farmer with a big straw hat, a pitchfork, and overalls would be a stereotype because not all farmers actually dress this way. Since stereotypes are often visual, like the farmer's hat, they gave comic book artists a lot of material to work with and can be found in almost every period of comic book history, especially in *The Invincible Iron Man*.

Regardless of the inaccuracy of these characters, or the negative depictions of Russia and China, the Cold War provided plenty of material for *Iron Man*'s writers. Whether the fans found these adventures thrilling or just plain ridiculous didn't matter much because either way, they appealed to thousands of avid comic book readers. Once again, it was part of the unpredictable, different approach that Marvel took with its comics.

5 IRON INFLUENCE

It is hard to tell how much influence *The Invincible Iron Man* has had on the comic book world. Marvel and the Marvel Universe, on the other hand, have had an enormous impact on the history of comics because of the style of the comic books they created. The Marvel Method, combined with Stan Lee's unique sense of humor, changed people's perceptions of Super Heroes and comic books in general.

Still, there are a few things about *Iron Man* in particular that make the comic stand out among its fellow Marvel titles and have likely helped inspire a new generation of artists and writers. A character who uses technology instead of superpowers was an entirely different way of looking at the traditional Super Hero. Tony Stark, with his multiple problems, helped reinvent what a comic book character could be. Iron

Man's technology and Stark's personality have consistently been two things comic fans have appreciated over the years.

ALWAYS ADVANCED

Iron Man's suit is the most significant technology used in the comic. Science fiction writers and real-world scientists alike have long been fascinated with the possibility of merging a person with mechanized armor similar to the type that Tony Stark wears. This combination of a person and advanced technological parts is called a cyborg. Tony Stark's chest plate, which is permanently attached to his body in order to keep his heart beating, makes him a cyborg because it is a mechanical object that is also part of his body.

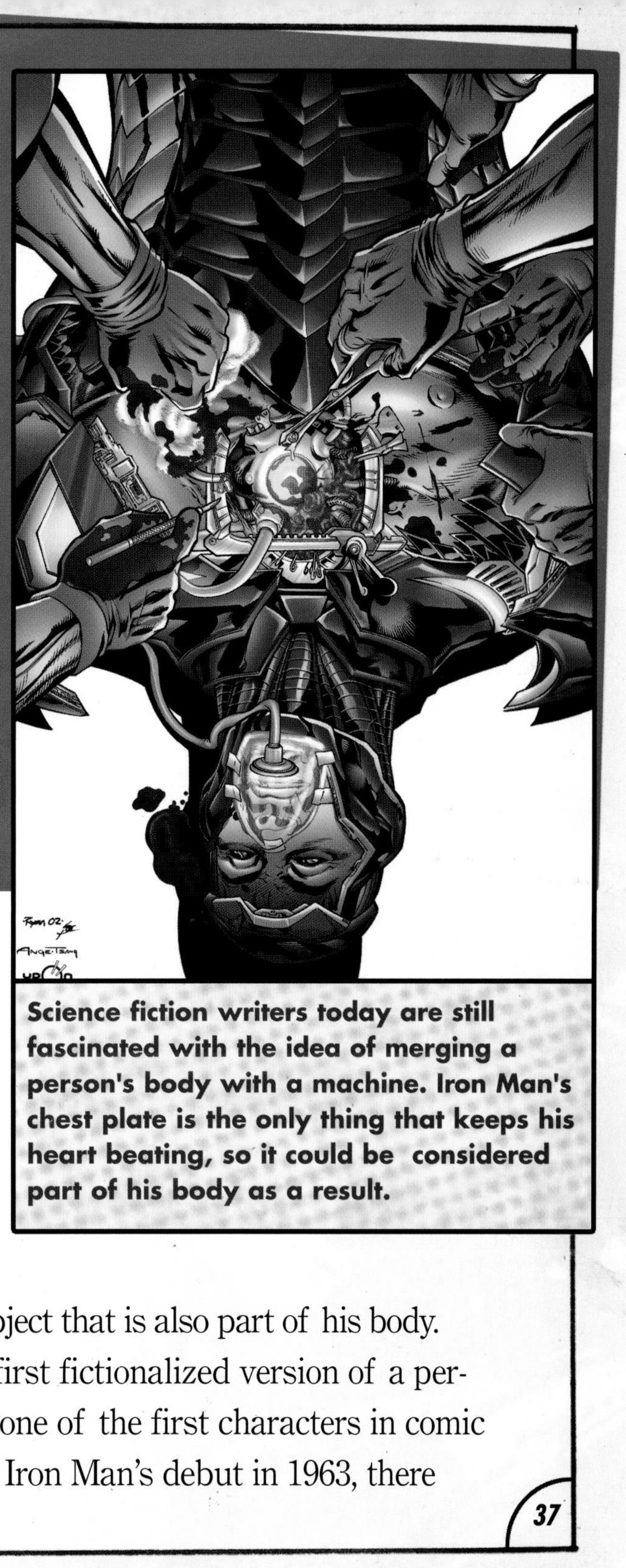

Science fiction writers today are still fascinated with the idea of merging a person's body with a machine. Iron Man's chest plate is the only thing that keeps his heart beating, so it could be considered part of his body as a result.

Although Iron Man is not the first fictionalized version of a person merging with a machine, he is one of the first characters in comic books to popularize the idea. Since Iron Man's debut in 1963, there have been hundreds of other characters in comic books, television, and the movies that have also been cyborgs. Darth Vader, the Borg from *Star Trek*, Robocop, and the Bionic Man are all cyborgs.

The armor featured in *Iron Man* is also technology that has been used by other writers. Shell Head's suit is different from a medieval knight's because his body controls his armor. If Tony

EXOSKELETONS

Unlike an insect or a lobster, which have a hard shell, humans need some help to make themselves stronger and more resistant to damage. The "help" comes in the form of a suit of armor called a human exoskeleton, and it is not unlike the suit Iron Man wears. A person wears the suit, and the suit responds to the movement of the body as if it were a part of the wearer's anatomy. For example, the strongest person in the world is not able to lift a car or truck up in the air. If he or she wears a powerful exoskeleton, however, he or she could potentially throw that same vehicle over his or her head. While the exoskeletons today are not quite this powerful, they are actively being researched by the military and are sometimes called battle armor or mobile suits. Japanese comics in particular have often shown characters wearing these types of suits, which they refer to as mecha.

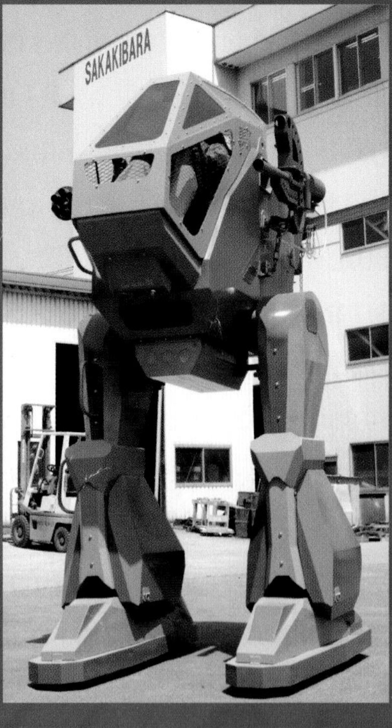
SAKAKIBARA

The human exoskeleton has long been a fixture of science fiction and comic books. A handful of real versions are in use today.

Stark squeezes his hand inside the suit, for example, then the hand of the armor also squeezes. The power of his clenching fist is amplified thousands of times and makes him incredibly strong. An armor that responds in this way is called a human exoskeleton.

Again, *Iron Man* wasn't the first work of fiction to feature this type of technology, but Iron Man was certainly one of the most popular characters to use it at the time. Now, many other comic book characters from all over the world have human exoskeletons. Exoskeletons are even being researched by real scientists for use in our world.

MADE OF FLESH

Above and beyond the technology featured in *Iron Man*, it is the character of Tony Stark that has probably had the biggest influence on the modern Super Hero. A character with flaws, some serious and undesirable, proved to create a more interesting comic book than one that merely featured a hero with superpowers.

It was character development that helped make the Marvel formula work back in 1963. It is what still drives the company's success today, both on the page and the big screen. Without something for a fan to care about besides how well the artwork is drawn or what the hero can do with his or her abilities, there isn't much to keep the reader interested. Conflict with an evil enemy, spy, or machine programmed to destroy the earth is fun to read about, but conflict with other people or within the characters themselves is something that doesn't require superpowers to understand.

TIMELINE: STAN LEE AND JACK KIRBY

1917 Jack Kirby is born.

1922 Stan Lee is born.

1936 Jack Kirby starts his comic book career for a company called Lincoln Newspaper Syndicate.

1940 Stan Lee starts work as an assistant for Timely Comics, which would eventually become Marvel Comics. First works with Jack Kirby as a gofer.

1940 *Captain America* is co-created by Jack Kirby and Joe Simon.

1945 Stan Lee enlists in the army and is stationed in Astoria, Queens.

Jack Kirby is drafted and fights in World War II. He spends most of his time in France and Germany on the front lines as a scout.

1950 Timely Publications becomes Atlas Comics.

1961 The first issue of *The Fantastic Four* is published.

1963 Timely changes its name to Marvel.

1970 Jack Kirby quits Marvel and joins DC.

1994 Jack Kirby dies.

IRON MAN HIGHLIGHTS

1963 Iron Man first appears in *Tales of Suspense* issue #39, featuring a cover drawn by Jack Kirby and interior art by Don Heck.

1964 Iron Man's armor changes to red and gold, the colors most fans associate him with.

1966 Iron Man makes his first television appearance in the Marvel Super Heroes animated series, which lasts for thirteen episodes.

1968 The first issue of *The Invincible Iron Man* is released.

1970–1971 Don Heck, who worked on the original *Tales of Suspense*, returns to work on the character he helped co-create.

1978–1982 Period during which Tony Stark develops a drinking problem that would continue to haunt him throughout his career as Iron Man.

1983 Jim Rhodes becomes Iron Man for the first time.

1987 Tony Stark tries to take back from the government some of the weapons he has developed and becomes seen as an enemy rather than a hero by the U.S. government.

1990 Famous *X-Men* artist John Byrne comes to work on *Iron Man*.

1994 As part of the Marvel Action Hour, Iron Man appears in a TV series along with the Fantastic Four. The show spawned a line of action figures.

1996 The last issue of *The Invincible Iron Man* is published. Later in the year, Iron Man reappears in a series called *Heroes Reborn*.

2005 *Iron Man*, the movie, begins preproduction with a scheduled release date of 2007.

GLOSSARY

anti-Semitism A prejudice against people of Jewish heritage.

Cold War A period of hostility and indirect conflict in the mid-twentieth century between the United States and the Soviet Union that affected diplomacy and economics.

comic panel The boxes drawn in comic books that artists use to create the visual part of the story.

comic strip A short series of drawings, used to tell a story or a joke.

cyborg A person whose body has been altered by using technology, such as replacing a missing hand with a robotic one.

exoskeleton A hard outer shell that provides support and protection for an organism, such as a lobster.

genre A type or category of an artistic creation, such as a mystery novel or an action movie.

industrialist A person who makes his or her living by producing or helping to produce products that are needed for industrial purposes, such as construction, the military, and machine manufacturers.

magnetism The force or energy created by magnets or magnetic fields.

stereotype A simplified or generalized view of a person based on his or her background. Stereotypes are often negative or prejudicial.

Cartoon Art Museum
655 Mission Street
San Francisco, CA 94105
(415) 227-8666
Web site: http://cartoonart.org

The Comic Book Project
Dr. Michael Bitz, Founder & Director
Teachers College, Columbia University
520A Horace Mann Hall, Box 139
525 West 120th Street
New York, NY 10027
(212) 330-7444
Web site: http://www.comicbookproject.org

New York City Comic Book Museum
P.O. Box 230676
New York, NY 10023
Web site: http://www.nyccomicbookmuseum.org/main.htm

WEB SITES

Due to the changing nature of Internet links, the Rosen
Publishing Group, Inc., has developed an online list of Web
sites related to the subject of this book. This site is updated
regularly. Please use the link below to access the list:
http://www.rosenlinks.com/crah/iron
You can also refer to the Marvel Web site:
http://www.marvel.com

FOR FURTHER READING

George, Milo, ed. *The Comics Journal Library, Volume One: Jack Kirby*. Seattle, WA: Fantagraphics, 2002.

Heck, Don, Stan Lee, et al. *The Essential Iron Man Volume One*. New York, NY: Marvel Comics, 2000.

Jones, Gerard. *Men of Tomorrow: Geeks, Gangsters, and the Birth of the Comic Book*. New York, NY: Basic Books, 2004.

Raphael, Jordon, and Tom Spurgeon. *Stan Lee and the Rise and Fall of the American Comic Book*. Chicago, IL: Chicago Review Press, 2003.

Ro, Ronin. *Tales to Astonish: Jack Kirby, Stan Lee, and the American Comic Book Revolution*. New York, NY: Bloomsbury, 2004.

BIBLIOGRAPHY

Card, Orson Scott. "Ultimate Iron Man." *Ultimate Iron Man*, Vol. 1, No. 1, May 2005.

Ellis, Warren. "Iron Man Extremis." *Iron Man*, Vol. 4, No. 1, January 2005.

George, Milo, ed. *The Comics Journal Library Volume One: Jack Kirby*. Seattle, WA: Fantagraphics Books, 2002.

Heck, Don, Stan Lee, et al. *The Essential Iron Man Volume One*. New York, NY: Marvel Comics, 2000.

Iron Man Armory. "The Invincible Iron Man." Retrieved June 20, 2005 (http://www.ironmanarmory.com).

Jones, Gerard. *Men of Tomorrow: Geeks, Gangsters and the Birth of the Comic Book*. New York, NY: Basic Books, 2004

Lee, Stan. *The Avengers* (Marvel Masterworks). Volume One. New York, NY: Marvel Entertainment Group, 1993.

Lee, Stan, and George Mair. *Excelsior: The Amazing Life of Stan Lee*. New York, NY: Fireside, 2002.

Lee, Stan. *Origins of Marvel Comics*. New York, NY: Simon and Schuster, 1974.

Lee, Stan. *Son of Origins of Marvel Comics*. New York, NY: Simon and Schuster, 1975.

Marvel Directory. "Iron Man." Retrieved June 20, 2005 (http://www.marveldirectory.com/individuals/i/ironman.htm).

Raphael, Jordon, and Tom Spurgeon. *Stan Lee and the Rise and Fall of the American Comic Book.* Chicago, IL: Chicago Review Press, 2003.

Ro, Ronin. *Tales to Astonish: Jack Kirby, Stan Lee, and the American Comic Book Revolution.* New York, NY: Bloomsbury, 2004.

Stone, Brad. "Ironmen." *Wired*, January 2005. Retrieved July 15, 2005 (http://www.wired.com/wired/archive/13.01/ironmen.html).

INDEX

A

anti-Semitism, 10
Atlas Comics, 10, 20
Avengers, the, 34

B

Batman, 12, 14
Byrne, John, 25

C

Captain America, 10, 12, 13, 28, 32, 34
Cold War, 32–33, 35
comics industry, problems in, 13–14, 27
cyborgs, 37–38

D

DC Comics, 14
Ditko, Steve, 25

E

exoskeleton, 38, 39

F

Fantastic Four, the, 14–15, 20, 28

G

Goodman, Martin, 9–10

H

Heck, Don, 23, 25

I

Invincible Iron Man, The, 6, 24, 27, 28, 30, 31, 32, 35, 36

Iron Man

appearance of, 7, 20–21
character development of, 6, 39
contributors to, 23, 25
evolution of, 7, 21, 25, 28
influence of, 36–39
debut of, 6, 15–17, 20–23
problems experienced by, 5–6, 7, 17, 25–26
storylines for, 21–23, 24, 25–26, 30, 34
technology and, 37–39
as Tony Stark, 5, 17, 21, 23, 25–27, 30–31, 34, 36, 39
wars and, 6–7, 21, 32–35

K

Kirby, Jack
childhood of, 8, 11–12
death of, 12
influence/importance of, 6, 10–11, 12, 14
Iron Man and, 6, 20, 23, 29–30
at Marvel, 10, 12, 19
start in comics, 12

L

Lee, Stan
childhood of, 8–9, 11
influence/importance of, 6, 14
Iron Man and, 6, 20, 23, 29–30
at Marvel, 10, 15, 17–19, 31–32, 34
new direction for comics and, 14
start in comics, 10
Lieber, Larry, 25

M

Marvel Comics
   influence/importance
      of, 19, 36, 39
      in 1960s, 5, 30, 39
Marvel Method, 15
Marvel Universe, 6, 15, 36
Michelinie, David, 25

S

Spider-Man, 25
stereotype, definition of, 35
Superman, 12, 14

T

Tales of Suspense, 20, 24, 25, 30, 32
Timely Publications, 10, 12

ABOUT THE AUTHOR

Adam Eisenberg lives in Brooklyn with his dog, Bullet. He has recently finished writing his first novel, which was inspired by the Marvel comics he read growing up. Once a month he still makes his ritual trip to the comic book store to check out the new releases.

PHOTO CREDITS

p. 9 © Joe Thomas/Getty Images; p. 11 courtesy of Lisa Kirby and © the Kirby Estate; p. 38 © AP/Wide World Photos. All other images provided by Marvel Entertainment, Inc.

Designer: Thomas Forget
Editor: Liz Gavril
Photo Researcher: Les Kanturek